My Peacock

Written by Pam Wallinger

Photographs by Bill Wallinger

A peacock came to my house.

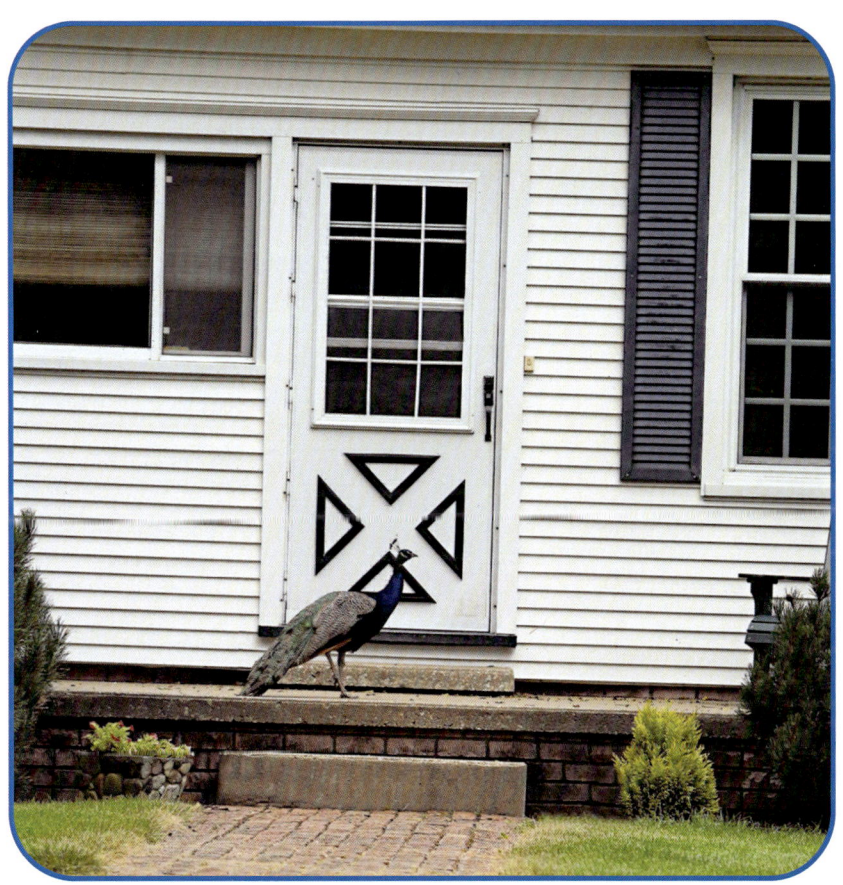

He walked in the grass.

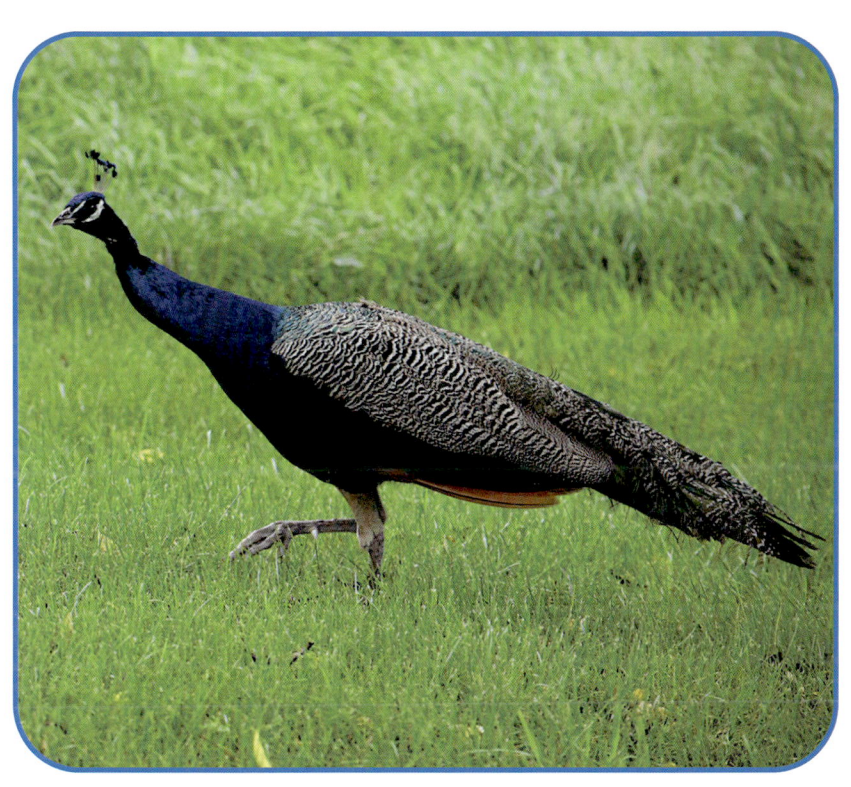

He sat on the fence.

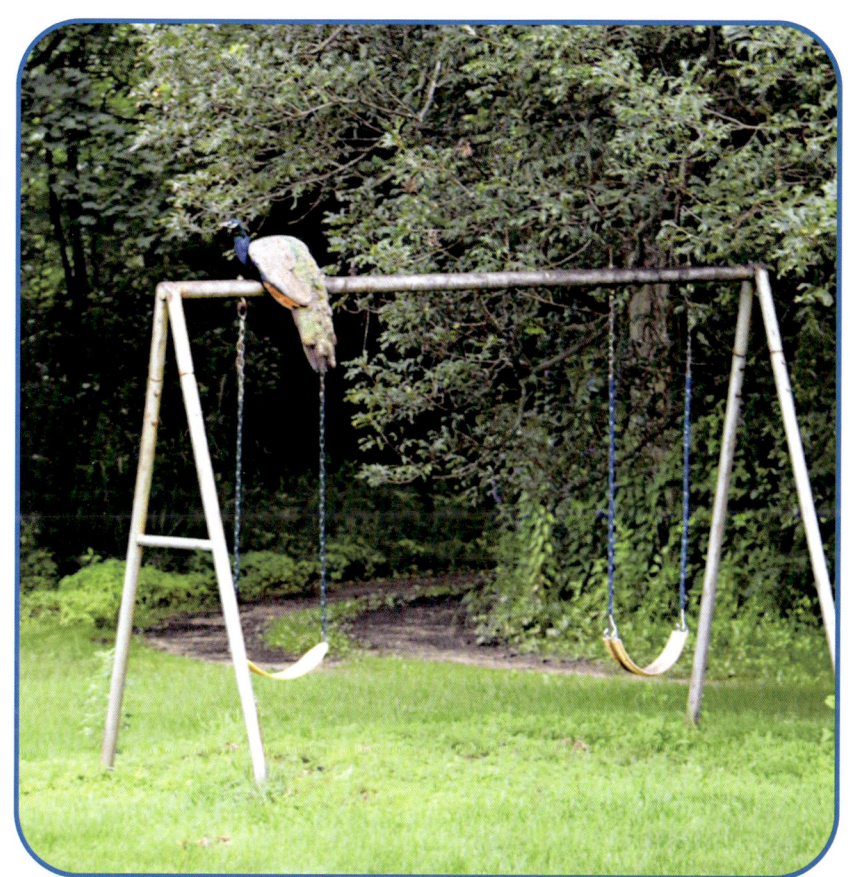

He looked at the flowers.

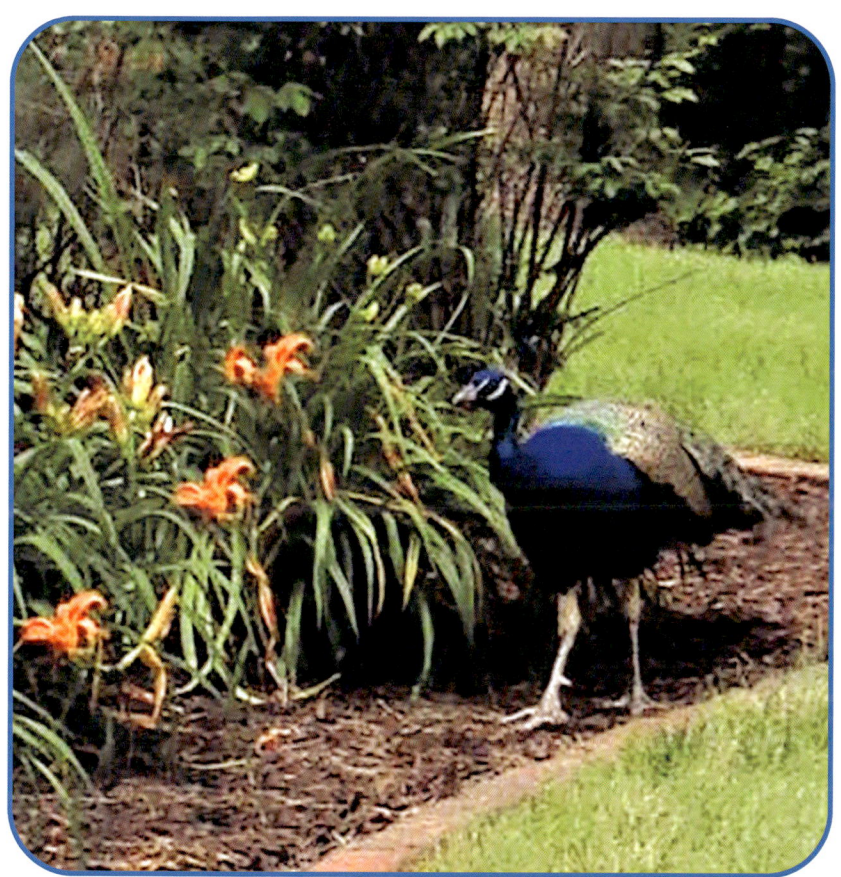

He sat on the porch.

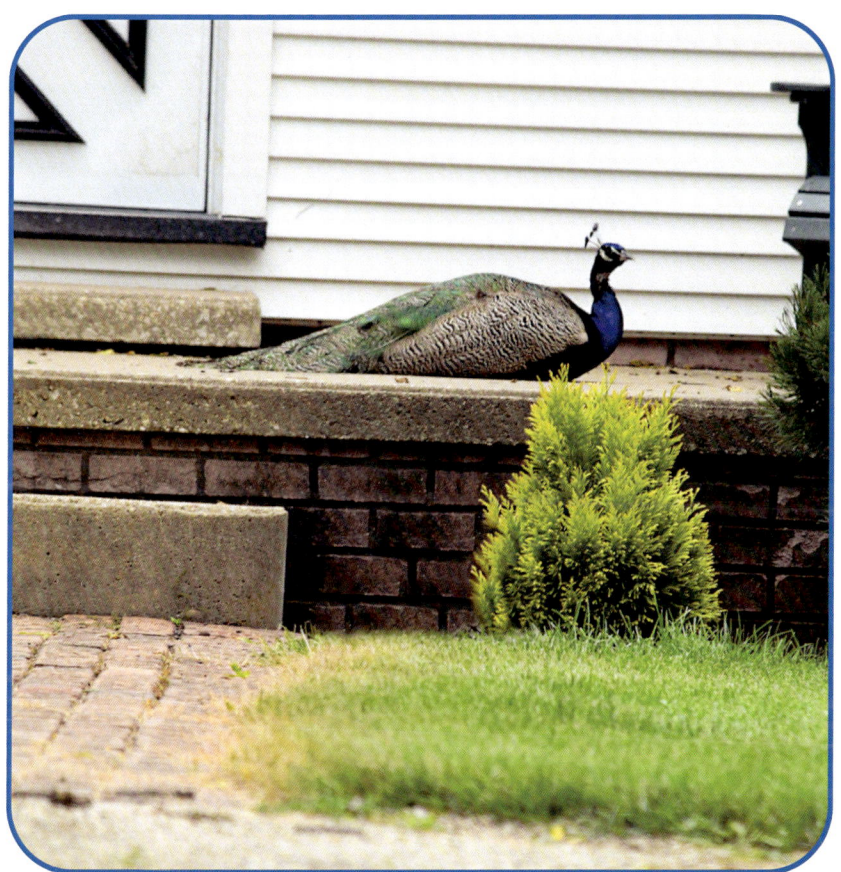

He walked into the leaves.

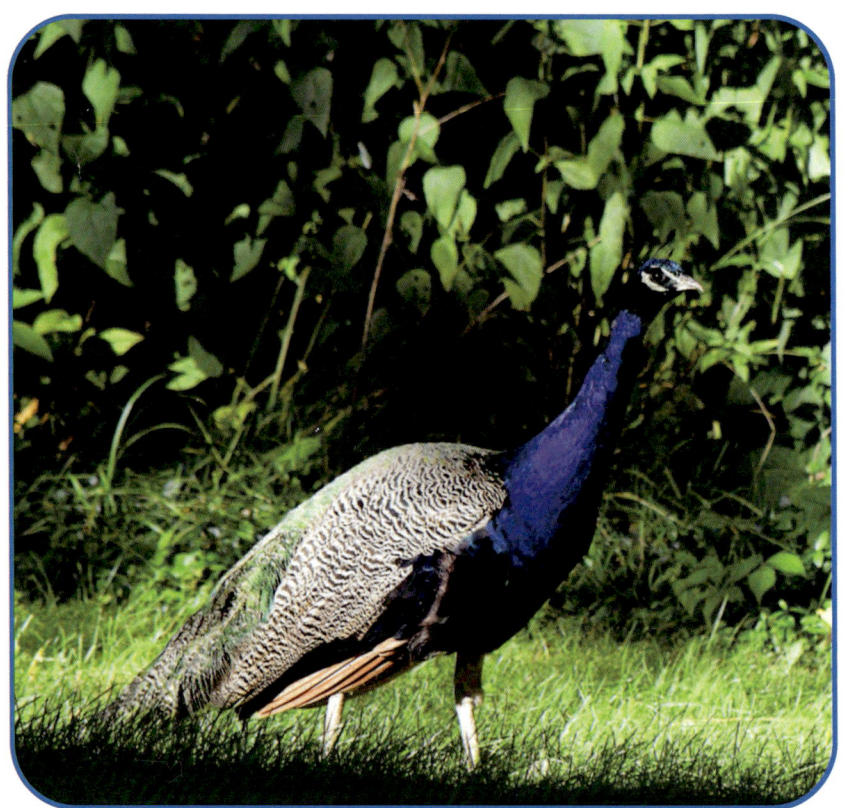